Broccoli Cheddar Soup Recipes

Delicious Variations and Creative Twists for the Classic Comfort Soup

While every precaution has been taken in the preparation of this book, the publisher assumes no responsibility for errors or omissions, or for damages resulting from the use of the information contained herein.

BROCCOLI CHEDDAR SOUP RECIPES

First edition. December 4, 2023.

Copyright © 2023 john ahmad.

ISBN: 979-8223215769

Written by john ahmad.

Table of Contents

John Ahmad

Chapter 1: Introduction to Broccoli Cheddar Soup

The Comfort of Broccoli Cheddar Soup

Few dishes offer the same level of warmth and comfort as a steaming bowl of broccoli cheddar soup. With its creamy texture, hearty flavors, and the perfect balance of vegetables and cheese, this soup has earned its place as a classic comfort food. In this chapter, we'll take a closer look at the essence of broccoli cheddar soup, its rich history, and the variations that make it a versatile and beloved choice for any occasion.

A Brief History of the Classic Dish

Broccoli cheddar soup, though widely enjoyed today, has a relatively recent origin. It gained popularity in the 20th century as a part of the broader movement of creating comforting and satisfying foods. Its roots can be traced back to the United States, where the combination of fresh broccoli and the creamy goodness of cheddar cheese quickly won the hearts of many. Since then, this soup has become a staple in homes, restaurants, and even fast-food chains, solidifying its place as an all-time favorite.

Key Ingredients and Variations

The beauty of broccoli cheddar soup lies in its simplicity and versatility. The two key ingredients, broccoli and cheddar cheese, form the foundation of the dish, but there's plenty of room for creativity and experimentation. Here are a few ways you can customize this classic soup:

Broccoli Variations: While traditional recipes call for standard broccoli florets, you can mix things up by using broccolini, Romanesco broccoli, or even purple broccoli for an unexpected twist in color and flavor.

Cheese Choices: Cheddar is the star of the show, but you can experiment with different types of cheddar—sharp, mild, white, or aged—for varying degrees of flavor. You could also blend in other cheeses like Gouda, Parmesan, or even blue cheese to add complexity.

Creaminess Factors: The creamy texture of the soup can be achieved using heavy cream, milk, or even alternatives like coconut milk for a dairy-free option. Greek yogurt can also add a tangy creaminess that balances the richness of the cheese.

Flavor Enhancements: Elevate the flavor profile by incorporating additional ingredients such as roasted garlic, caramelized onions, or a touch of smoky paprika. These elements can take the soup's taste to new heights.

Garnishes and Toppings: Don't forget the finishing touches! Crumbled bacon, herbed croutons, a drizzle of truffle oil, or a sprinkle of chopped fresh herbs can all enhance the visual appeal and taste of your soup.

In the upcoming chapters, we'll delve deeper into these variations and more, providing you with step-by-step instructions and tips to create each version of broccoli cheddar soup. Whether you're looking for a classic rendition or an inventive twist on the original, this cookbook has you covered.

With a foundation of rich history, comforting flavors, and the potential for creative culinary exploration, broccoli cheddar soup is not just a dish—it's an experience. So, roll up your sleeves, gather your ingredients, and get ready to embark on a journey of flavor, comfort, and culinary delight.

Feel free to immerse yourself in the chapters ahead, as we dive into the delightful world of "Broccoli Cheddar Soup Recipes." From classic renditions to unexpected twists, there's something here to satisfy every palate and occasion.

Chapter 2: The Basics of Making Perfect Broccoli Cheddar Soup

Essential Tools and Utensils

Before embarking on your journey to create the perfect broccoli cheddar soup, it's essential to have the right tools and utensils at your disposal. These items will not only make the cooking process smoother but also ensure that your soup turns out as delicious as you envision.

1. Soup Pot: A sturdy and appropriately sized soup pot is a must-have. It should be large enough to accommodate the ingredients comfortably without overcrowding.

2. Cutting Board and Knife: A reliable cutting board and a sharp chef's knife are essential for preparing the broccoli and other vegetables with precision.

3. Wooden Spoon: A wooden spoon is great for stirring the soup while it cooks, as it won't scratch the surface of your pot.

4. Immersion Blender or Stand Blender: Depending on your preference, an immersion blender (also known as a stick blender) or a stand blender will help you achieve the desired creamy consistency.

5. Ladle: A ladle makes it easy to transfer the soup from the pot to bowls without making a mess.

6. Measuring Cups and Spoons: Accurate measurements are crucial for achieving the right balance of flavors. Keep measuring cups and spoons handy.

7. Cheese Grater: For freshly grated cheese, a good-quality cheese grater is essential.

8. Wooden Chopping Board: This board can be dedicated to slicing and chopping vegetables to avoid cross-contamination with raw meats.

Selecting Fresh Ingredients

The quality of your ingredients greatly influences the taste and texture of your broccoli cheddar soup. Here's how to choose the best components for a delicious outcome:

1. Broccoli: opt for firm broccoli heads with tightly closed florets and vibrant green color. Avoid any signs of yellowing or wilting.

2. Cheddar Cheese: Choose a high-quality cheddar cheese with good flavor. If possible, purchase a block of cheese and grate it yourself for optimal freshness.

3. Onions and Garlic: Choose firm onions with dry, papery skins. Look for plump garlic bulbs with unblemished cloves.

4. Liquid Ingredients: If using milk, choose whole milk or cream for a rich and creamy base. If using broth, opt for a high-quality vegetable or chicken broth.

Step-by-Step Cooking Process

Creating a perfect pot of broccoli cheddar soup involves several steps that come together to produce a delicious and satisfying dish. Here's a step-by-step guide to help you along the way:

1. Prepare the Ingredients: Wash and chop the broccoli into bite-sized florets. Dice the onions and mince the garlic. Grate the cheddar cheese if not already grated.

2. Sauté the Aromatics: In your soup pot, heat a bit of oil or butter over medium heat. Add the diced onions and sauté until they become translucent. Add the minced garlic and sauté briefly until fragrant.

3. Cook the Broccoli: Add the broccoli florets to the pot and sauté for a few minutes, allowing them to slightly soften and absorb the flavors of the aromatics.

4. Make the Roux: Sprinkle a small amount of flour over the cooked vegetables and stir to create a roux. This will help thicken the soup.

5. Add Liquid: Gradually pour in your choice of liquid—milk, cream, or broth—while stirring constantly to prevent lumps from forming.

6. Simmer and Blend: Allow the mixture to simmer until the broccoli is tender. Then, either use an immersion blender or transfer the mixture to a stand blender to puree until smooth.

7. Add Cheese: Gradually add the grated cheddar cheese to the blended soup, stirring until fully melted and incorporated.

8. Season and Serve: Taste the soup and season with salt and pepper as needed. Ladle the soup into bowls and consider garnishing with additional cheese, chopped herbs, or croutons.

By mastering these fundamental techniques, you're well on your way to creating a perfectly balanced and creamy broccoli cheddar soup. As you gain confidence, feel free to experiment with the variations explored in the upcoming chapters. With practice, you'll be able to tailor this classic dish to your taste preferences and create a soup that brings comfort and joy with every spoonful

Chapter 3: Classic Creamy Broccoli Cheddar Soup

Traditional Recipe Walkthrough

Indulge in the timeless comfort of a classic creamy broccoli cheddar soup. This recipe pays homage to the original combination of tender broccoli and rich cheddar cheese, resulting in a velvety and satisfying bowl of goodness.

Ingredients:

- 2 tablespoons butter
- 1 medium onion, diced
- 2 cloves garlic, minced
- 4 cups broccoli florets
- 3 cups vegetable or chicken broth
- 2 cups whole milk or heavy cream
- 2 cups shredded sharp cheddar cheese
- Salt and pepper to taste

Instructions:

1. Sauté the Aromatics: In a large soup pot, melt the butter over medium heat. Add the diced onion and sauté until translucent, about 3-4 minutes. Stir in the minced garlic and sauté for an additional 1-2 minutes until fragrant.
2. Cook the Broccoli: Add the broccoli florets to the pot and sauté with the aromatics for about 5 minutes, allowing the flavors to meld.
3. Add Liquid: Pour in the vegetable or chicken broth, ensuring that it covers the broccoli. Bring the mixture to a gentle boil, then reduce the heat to a simmer. Let it simmer for about 15-20 minutes, or until the broccoli is tender.

4. Blend the Mixture: Use an immersion blender directly in the pot or transfer the mixture to a stand blender (in batches if necessary). Blend until the soup is smooth and creamy.

5. Incorporate Dairy: Return the blended mixture to the pot if using a stand blender. Pour in the whole milk or heavy cream, stirring to combine.

6. Add Cheese: Gradually add the shredded cheddar cheese, stirring continuously until the cheese is fully melted and the soup is creamy.

7. Season and Serve: Taste the soup and season with salt and pepper as needed. Keep in mind that the cheese adds saltiness, so adjust accordingly.

Tips for Achieving Creaminess

Blending Technique: To achieve optimal creaminess, blend the soup until completely smooth. This ensures that there are no chunks of broccoli remaining and that the cheese is evenly distributed.

Cheese Consistency: Shred your own cheddar cheese from a block for the best results. Pre-shredded cheese often contains additives that can affect the texture of the soup.

Consistent Heat: Maintain a gentle simmer when cooking the broccoli to ensure that it cooks evenly and becomes tender.

Add Dairy Gradually: When incorporating the dairy into the soup, add it slowly while stirring to prevent curdling and to achieve a smooth, velvety texture.

Serving and Garnishing Ideas

The classic creamy broccoli cheddar soup is versatile and can be customized to your taste. Here are some serving and garnishing ideas to enhance your dining experience:

Garnishes: Top your soup with a sprinkle of extra shredded cheddar cheese, a dollop of sour cream, or a drizzle of olive oil for a finishing touch.

Crunchy Texture: Add a contrast in texture with homemade croutons, crispy bacon bits, or toasted pumpkin seeds.

Fresh Herbs: Garnish with chopped fresh parsley, chives, or thyme to add a burst of color and a touch of freshness.

Bread Bowl: Serve the soup in hollowed-out bread bowls for a rustic and interactive dining experience.

Pairing: Accompany your soup with a crusty baguette or a side salad for a well-rounded meal.

Embrace the Comfort:

A bowl of classic creamy broccoli cheddar soup is a bowl of comfort, reminiscent of cherished memories and the simple joy of savoring familiar flavors. Whether enjoyed as a starter, a main course, or a soothing pick-me-up, this classic rendition of the soup will never fail to warm your heart and palate.

Chapter 4: Roasted Broccoli and Aged Cheddar Soup

Roasting Broccoli for Flavor

Elevate the traditional broccoli cheddar soup by infusing it with the deep and nutty flavors of roasted broccoli. Roasting not only intensifies the taste of the broccoli but also adds a delightful smokiness that takes this classic dish to new heights.

Ingredients:

- 4 cups broccoli florets
- 2 tablespoons olive oil
- Salt and pepper to taste

Instructions:

1. Preheat the Oven: Preheat your oven to 400°F (200°C).
2. Prepare the Broccoli: Toss the broccoli florets with olive oil, ensuring they are evenly coated. Sprinkle with salt and pepper to taste.
3. Roast the Broccoli: Spread the broccoli florets in a single layer on a baking sheet. Roast in the preheated oven for about 20-25 minutes, or until the edges are slightly crispy and the broccoli is tender.
4. Cool and Set Aside: Allow the roasted broccoli to cool slightly before using it in the soup. This step prevents the hot broccoli from causing steam when blended.

Incorporating Aged Cheddar's Richness

Aged cheddar brings a complexity of flavor to this roasted broccoli soup. Its sharpness and depth perfectly complement the roasted notes of the broccoli, resulting in a soup that's both comforting and sophisticated.

Ingredients:

- Roasted broccoli (prepared from the previous section)
- 2 tablespoons butter
- 1 medium onion, diced
- 2 cloves garlic, minced
- 4 cups vegetable or chicken broth
- 1 cup whole milk or heavy cream
- 2 cups shredded aged cheddar cheese
- Salt and pepper to taste

Instructions:

1. Sauté the Aromatics: In a large soup pot, melt the butter over medium heat. Add the diced onion and sauté until translucent, about 3-4 minutes. Stir in the minced garlic and sauté for an additional 1-2 minutes until fragrant.
2. Blend Roasted Broccoli: Add the roasted broccoli to the pot, reserving a small amount for garnish. Stir to combine with the aromatics.
3. Add Liquid: Pour in the vegetable or chicken broth, ensuring it covers the broccoli mixture. Bring to a gentle boil, then reduce the heat and let it simmer for about 15 minutes.
4. Blend and Add Dairy: Use an immersion blender or a stand blender to blend the mixture until smooth. Return it to the pot if necessary. Pour in the whole milk or heavy cream, stirring to combine.
5. Incorporate Aged Cheddar: Gradually add the shredded aged cheddar cheese, stirring until fully melted and incorporated.
6. Season and Serve: Taste the soup and season with salt and

pepper as needed. Keep in mind that the cheese adds saltiness, so adjust accordingly.

Enhancing Texture and Taste

Achieving the perfect texture and taste in your roasted broccoli and aged cheddar soup requires attention to detail. Here are some tips to help you create a soup that's both visually appealing and incredibly satisfying:

Blend Smoothly: When blending the soup, aim for a velvety-smooth consistency. This will ensure a uniform distribution of flavors and a luxurious mouthfeel.

Reserve Garnishes: Set aside a small portion of the roasted broccoli for garnishing each bowl. The contrast between the blended soup and the tender florets will enhance the presentation.

Serve with Crispy Elements: For added texture, consider topping each serving with crispy bacon bits or croutons. These elements not only provide a satisfying crunch but also offer a delightful contrast to the creamy base.

Savor the Depth: Aged cheddar imparts a distinctive depth of flavor to the soup. Allow yourself to savor the nuances of the cheese, which will shine through the roasted broccoli and create a harmonious taste experience.

By embracing the roasted flavors of the broccoli and the rich essence of aged cheddar, you'll create a soup that captivates the senses with each spoonful. This variation celebrates the art of blending flavors and textures to create a dish that's both familiar and excitingly new.

Chapter 5: Healthy Broccoli Cheddar Soup with Greek Yogurt

Healthier Ingredient Substitutions

Elevate your broccoli cheddar soup to a healthier level without sacrificing taste by incorporating Greek yogurt. This variation retains all the comforting flavors you love while introducing a wholesome twist that's as nourishing as it is delicious.

Ingredients:

- 2 tablespoons olive oil
- 1 medium onion, diced
- 2 cloves garlic, minced
- 4 cups broccoli florets
- 3 cups vegetable or chicken broth
- 1 cup water
- 1 cup plain Greek yogurt
- 1 ½ cups shredded sharp cheddar cheese
- Salt and pepper to taste

Instructions:

1. Sauté the Aromatics: In a large soup pot, heat the olive oil over medium heat. Add the diced onion and sauté until translucent, about 3-4 minutes. Stir in the minced garlic and sauté for an additional 1-2 minutes until fragrant.
2. Cook the Broccoli: Add the broccoli florets to the pot and sauté with the aromatics for about 5 minutes, allowing the flavors to meld.
3. Add Liquid: Pour in the vegetable or chicken broth and water. Bring the mixture to a gentle boil, then reduce the heat to a simmer. Let it simmer for about 15-20 minutes, or until the

broccoli is tender.

4. Blend the Mixture: Use an immersion blender or transfer the mixture to a stand blender to puree until smooth.

5. Incorporate Greek Yogurt: Once the soup is smooth, temper the Greek yogurt by gradually adding a small amount of the hot soup to the yogurt, stirring constantly to prevent curdling. Then, slowly whisk the tempered yogurt into the pot.

6. Add Cheese: Gradually add the shredded cheddar cheese to the soup, stirring until fully melted and incorporated.

7. Season and Serve: Taste the soup and season with salt and pepper as needed.

Creaminess with Greek Yogurt

Greek yogurt offers a creamy and tangy alternative to heavy cream, providing a luscious texture that perfectly complements the flavors of broccoli and cheddar. Here's how to make the most of this wholesome substitution:

Tempering Technique: Tempering the Greek yogurt ensures that it integrates smoothly into the soup without curdling. This technique involves gradually introducing a small amount of the hot soup to the yogurt to adjust its temperature before adding it to the pot.

Balanced Tanginess: The tangy notes of Greek yogurt balance the richness of the cheese and contribute a pleasant and refreshing zing to the soup.

Creaminess Enhancement: Greek yogurt contributes to the soup's overall creaminess while reducing the saturated fat content compared to traditional heavy cream.

Nutritional Benefits of the Recipe

Embracing Greek yogurt in your broccoli cheddar soup introduces a range of nutritional benefits that enhance its overall appeal:

Protein Boost: Greek yogurt is rich in protein, contributing to a more satiating and satisfying meal.

Probiotic Goodness: Greek yogurt contains probiotics, which can support digestive health and a strong immune system.

Calcium Content: Both cheese and Greek yogurt are excellent sources of calcium, promoting healthy bones and teeth.

Reduced Fat: By using Greek yogurt instead of heavy cream, you reduce the saturated fat content while maintaining a creamy texture.

Nutrient-Rich Broccoli: Broccoli is packed with vitamins, minerals, and dietary fiber, making it a nutrient powerhouse.

By making this healthy broccoli cheddar soup with Greek yogurt, you're not only treating yourself to a delicious meal but also providing your body with essential nutrients and a balanced dose of creamy comfort.

Chapter 6: Spicy Jalapeno and Cheddar Broccoli Soup

Adding Heat with Jalapenos

Turn up the heat and infuse your broccoli cheddar soup with a fiery twist by introducing the bold flavor of jalapenos. This variation takes your taste buds on a spicy adventure while keeping the comforting essence of the classic soup intact.

Ingredients:

- 2 tablespoons olive oil
- 1 medium onion, diced
- 2 cloves garlic, minced
- 4 cups broccoli florets
- 2 jalapeno peppers, seeds removed and diced
- 3 cups vegetable or chicken broth
- 2 cups whole milk or heavy cream
- 1 ½ cups shredded sharp cheddar cheese
- Salt and pepper to taste

Instructions:

1. Sauté the Aromatics: Heat the olive oil in a large soup pot over medium heat. Add the diced onion and sauté until translucent, about 3-4 minutes. Stir in the minced garlic and diced jalapenos, and sauté for an additional 1-2 minutes until fragrant.
2. Cook the Broccoli: Add the broccoli florets to the pot and sauté with the aromatics for about 5 minutes, allowing the flavors to meld.
3. Add Liquid: Pour in the vegetable or chicken broth, ensuring it covers the broccoli mixture. Bring to a gentle boil, then reduce

the heat to a simmer. Let it simmer for about 15-20 minutes, or until the broccoli is tender.

4. Blend the Mixture: Use an immersion blender or transfer the mixture to a stand blender to puree until smooth.

5. Incorporate Dairy: Once the soup is smooth, return it to the pot if necessary. Pour in the whole milk or heavy cream, stirring to combine.

6. Add Cheese: Gradually add the shredded cheddar cheese to the soup, stirring until fully melted and incorporated.

7. Season and Serve: Taste the soup and season with salt and pepper as needed. Keep in mind that the cheese adds saltiness, so adjust accordingly.

Balancing Spice and Flavor

Achieving the right balance of spice and flavor in a jalapeno-infused soup requires a thoughtful approach. Here are some tips to ensure your soup delivers the desired kick without overwhelming the palate:

Adjust Jalapeno Quantity: The number of jalapenos you use will determine the heat level of the soup. You can start with one jalapeno for a milder kick and increase the quantity if you prefer more heat.

Remove Seeds and Membranes: To control the spiciness, remove the seeds and membranes from the jalapenos before dicing them. The seeds and membranes contain most of the heat.

Taste and Adjust: Taste the soup as you add the diced jalapenos, keeping in mind that their spiciness can vary. This will help you gauge the desired level of heat.

Serving Suggestions for a Kick

When serving a jalapeno-spiced broccoli cheddar soup, consider complementing its fiery flavor with these exciting serving ideas:

Tortilla Strips: Top the soup with crispy tortilla strips for a Tex-Mex-inspired crunch that enhances the spicy profile.

Sour Cream: A dollop of sour cream or Greek yogurt can offer a cooling contrast to the heat while adding a creamy element.

Fresh Lime: A squeeze of fresh lime juice just before serving brightens the flavors and provides a zesty balance to the spiciness.

Avocado Slices: Creamy avocado slices not only provide richness but also help temper the heat for a well-rounded taste experience.

By embracing the boldness of jalapenos in your broccoli cheddar soup, you're creating a dish that satisfies spice lovers and comfort seekers alike. The interplay of heat and creamy indulgence makes this variation a memorable addition to your culinary repertoire.

Chapter 7: Broccoli Cheddar Soup with Bacon Bits

Infusing Smoky Bacon Flavor

Elevate your broccoli cheddar soup with the irresistible allure of smoky bacon. The combination of tender broccoli, rich cheddar cheese, and the savory goodness of crispy bacon creates a symphony of flavors that's nothing short of sensational.

Ingredients:

- 4 slices bacon
- 2 tablespoons butter
- 1 medium onion, diced
- 2 cloves garlic, minced
- 4 cups broccoli florets
- 3 cups vegetable or chicken broth
- 2 cups whole milk or heavy cream
- 1 ½ cups shredded sharp cheddar cheese
- Salt and pepper to taste

Instructions:

1. Cook the Bacon: In a skillet over medium heat, cook the bacon until crispy. Remove the bacon from the skillet, drain on paper towels, and crumble into small pieces. Set aside.
2. Sauté the Aromatics: In a large soup pot, melt the butter over medium heat. Add the diced onion and sauté until translucent, about 3-4 minutes. Stir in the minced garlic and sauté for an additional 1-2 minutes until fragrant.
3. Cook the Broccoli: Add the broccoli florets to the pot and sauté with the aromatics for about 5 minutes, allowing the flavors to meld.

4. Add Liquid: Pour in the vegetable or chicken broth, ensuring it covers the broccoli mixture. Bring to a gentle boil, then reduce the heat to a simmer. Let it simmer for about 15-20 minutes, or until the broccoli is tender.
5. Blend the Mixture: Use an immersion blender or transfer the mixture to a stand blender to puree until smooth.
6. Incorporate Dairy: Once the soup is smooth, return it to the pot if necessary. Pour in the whole milk or heavy cream, stirring to combine.
7. Add Cheese and Bacon: Gradually add the shredded cheddar cheese to the soup, stirring until fully melted and incorporated. Reserve a portion of the crumbled bacon for garnish and stir the rest into the soup.
8. Season and Serve: Taste the soup and season with salt and pepper as needed. Keep in mind that the cheese and bacon add saltiness, so adjust accordingly.

Cooking Crispy Bacon Toppings

Crispy bacon toppings are a must when serving bacon-infused broccoli cheddar soup. Here's how to achieve perfectly crispy bacon pieces for that ultimate smoky finish:

Choose Quality Bacon: Opt for thick-cut bacon with a good balance of meat and fat for the best results.

Cooking Technique: Cook the bacon in a skillet over medium heat until it turns crispy and golden brown. This will take about 5-7 minutes. Ensure you flip the bacon slices occasionally for even cooking.

Drain and Cool: Once the bacon is cooked to your desired crispness, remove it from the skillet and place it on a plate lined with paper towels. The paper towels will absorb excess grease.

Crumble with Care: Allow the cooked bacon to cool slightly before crumbling it into small pieces. This step prevents you from burning your fingers and ensures even crumbles.

Combining Savory Elements

The marriage of savory bacon, velvety cheese, and tender broccoli in this variation creates a harmonious blend of flavors that's both comforting and indulgent:

Umami Depth: The smokiness of the bacon adds a layer of umami that enhances the overall richness of the soup.

Texture Contrast: The crispy bacon bits provide a delightful contrast in texture to the creamy soup base, adding a satisfying crunch to each spoonful.

Balanced Salinity: Both the cheese and the bacon contribute saltiness to the dish. Taste the soup before adding additional salt to ensure a well-balanced flavor profile.

By incorporating bacon into your broccoli cheddar soup, you're infusing it with a smoky aroma and a savory dimension that's sure to delight your taste buds. This variation captures the essence of comfort food while introducing a touch of gourmet flair.

Chapter 8: Vegan "Cheesy" Broccoli Soup with Nutritional Yeast

Plant-Based Cheesy Flavor

Indulge in the rich and savory flavors of "cheesy" broccoli soup even on a vegan or dairy-free diet. This variation uses the magic of nutritional yeast to capture the essence of cheddar cheese, providing a delightful plant-based alternative that's both satisfying and wholesome.

Ingredients:

- 2 tablespoons olive oil
- 1 medium onion, diced
- 2 cloves garlic, minced
- 4 cups broccoli florets
- 3 cups vegetable broth
- 2 cups unsweetened almond milk or other non-dairy milk
- ½ cup raw cashews, soaked and drained
- ¼ cup nutritional yeast
- 2 tablespoons lemon juice
- Salt and pepper to taste

Instructions:

1. Sauté the Aromatics: Heat the olive oil in a large soup pot over medium heat. Add the diced onion and sauté until translucent, about 3-4 minutes. Stir in the minced garlic and sauté for an additional 1-2 minutes until fragrant.
2. Cook the Broccoli: Add the broccoli florets to the pot and sauté with the aromatics for about 5 minutes, allowing the flavors to meld.
3. Add Liquid: Pour in the vegetable broth and non-dairy milk. Bring the mixture to a gentle boil, then reduce the heat to a

simmer. Let it simmer for about 15-20 minutes, or until the broccoli is tender.

4. Blend the Mixture: Use an immersion blender or transfer the mixture to a stand blender to puree until smooth.

5. Prepare Cashew Cream: In a high-speed blender, blend the soaked and drained cashews with a splash of water until you achieve a smooth and creamy consistency.

6. Incorporate Nutritional Yeast: Add the nutritional yeast and cashew cream to the soup, stirring to combine.

7. Add Lemon Juice: Stir in the lemon juice to brighten the flavors and add a tangy element that complements the "cheesy" profile.

8. Season and Serve: Taste the soup and season with salt and pepper as needed.

Nutritional Yeast as a Secret Ingredient

Nutritional yeast is a star ingredient in this vegan "cheesy" broccoli soup, providing a robust flavor reminiscent of cheddar cheese. Here's why nutritional yeast deserves a spot in your culinary repertoire:

Cheesy Umami: Nutritional yeast offers a natural umami quality that mimics the savory richness of cheese.

Vitamin B12: Nutritional yeast is often fortified with vitamin B12, making it a valuable source of this essential nutrient for those following a plant-based diet.

Creaminess Enhancement: When blended with cashews, nutritional yeast contributes to a creamy texture that closely resembles the mouthfeel of dairy-based soups.

Catering to Vegan and Dairy-Free Diets

By embracing nutritional yeast and plant-based ingredients, you're creating a soup that caters to vegan and dairy-free diets while delivering on taste and satisfaction:

Cashew Cream: Soaked and blended cashews provide a dairy-free alternative to heavy cream, adding creaminess without compromising on taste.

Non-Dairy Milk: Opt for unsweetened almond milk, coconut milk, or any other non-dairy milk of your choice to achieve a luscious texture.

Balancing Flavors: Lemon juice not only brightens the flavors but also balances the richness of the "cheesy" profile, creating a harmonious taste experience.

Nutrient-Rich Broccoli: The addition of broccoli ensures that your soup is packed with vitamins, minerals, and fiber, contributing to a well-rounded and nourishing meal.

By creating a vegan "cheesy" broccoli soup with nutritional yeast, you're crafting a dish that celebrates both innovation and tradition. This variation embraces the culinary possibilities of plant-based ingredients while maintaining the essence of comfort and flavor that makes broccoli cheddar soup a beloved classic.

Chapter 9: Broccoli Cheddar Soup with a Twist of Beer

Incorporating Beer for Depth

Elevate your broccoli cheddar soup with a unique twist by infusing it with the complex and rich flavors of beer. This variation introduces a layer of depth that perfectly complements the creamy essence of the soup, resulting in a delightful harmony of taste.

Ingredients:

- 2 tablespoons butter
- 1 medium onion, diced
- 2 cloves garlic, minced
- 4 cups broccoli florets
- 3 cups vegetable or chicken broth
- 1 cup beer (choose a style that complements the flavors)
- 2 cups whole milk or heavy cream
- 1 ½ cups shredded sharp cheddar cheese
- Salt and pepper to taste

Instructions:

1. Sauté the Aromatics: In a large soup pot, melt the butter over medium heat. Add the diced onion and sauté until translucent, about 3-4 minutes. Stir in the minced garlic and sauté for an additional 1-2 minutes until fragrant.
2. Cook the Broccoli: Add the broccoli florets to the pot and sauté with the aromatics for about 5 minutes, allowing the flavors to meld.
3. Add Liquid: Pour in the vegetable or chicken broth and beer. Choose a beer style that complements the flavors of the soup; consider options like a light lager, pale ale, or even a stout for

a richer taste. Bring the mixture to a gentle boil, then reduce the heat to a simmer. Let it simmer for about 15-20 minutes, or until the broccoli is tender.

4. Blend the Mixture: Use an immersion blender or transfer the mixture to a stand blender to puree until smooth.

5. Incorporate Dairy: Once the soup is smooth, return it to the pot if necessary. Pour in the whole milk or heavy cream, stirring to combine.

6. Add Cheese: Gradually add the shredded cheddar cheese to the soup, stirring until fully melted and incorporated.

7. Season and Serve: Taste the soup and season with salt and pepper as needed. Keep in mind that the cheese adds saltiness, so adjust accordingly.

Best Beer Styles for the Recipe

Selecting the right beer style is crucial for achieving a harmonious fusion of flavors. Here are some beer styles that pair well with the elements of broccoli cheddar soup:

Light Lager: A light and crisp lager can enhance the overall flavors without overpowering the dish.

Pale Ale: The citrusy and slightly bitter notes of a pale ale can complement the richness of the cheddar cheese and add a refreshing touch.

Stout or Porter: For a more robust and hearty version, consider a stout or porter, which can contribute deep roasted flavors that blend beautifully with the creamy soup.

Cooking Off Alcohol while Retaining Flavor

While beer adds a unique flavor dimension to the soup, it's important to cook off the alcohol to ensure a balanced taste. Here's how to retain the essence of the beer while reducing its alcoholic content:

Simmering: Simmer the soup after adding the beer to allow the alcohol to evaporate gradually. This step helps retain the beer's flavor while minimizing its alcoholic potency.

Flavor Development: Cooking the beer enhances its flavors, and those complex notes will be integrated into the soup even after the alcohol content has decreased.

By embracing the rich flavors of beer in your broccoli cheddar soup, you're creating a variation that's both sophisticated and comforting. The marriage of creamy textures and nuanced beer undertones offers a culinary experience that's sure to intrigue and delight your taste buds.

Chapter 10: Smoky Gouda and Broccoli Soup

Exploring Gouda's Smokiness

Embark on a culinary journey with a smoky twist by infusing your broccoli cheddar soup with the distinctive flavors of Gouda cheese. The rich and smoky essence of Gouda lends a unique and captivating dimension to this beloved classic.

Ingredients:

- 2 tablespoons butter
- 1 medium onion, diced
- 2 cloves garlic, minced
- 4 cups broccoli florets
- 3 cups vegetable or chicken broth
- 2 cups whole milk or heavy cream
- 1 ½ cups shredded Gouda cheese
- Salt and pepper to taste

Instructions:

1. Sauté the Aromatics: In a large soup pot, melt the butter over medium heat. Add the diced onion and sauté until translucent, about 3-4 minutes. Stir in the minced garlic and sauté for an additional 1-2 minutes until fragrant.
2. Cook the Broccoli: Add the broccoli florets to the pot and sauté with the aromatics for about 5 minutes, allowing the flavors to meld.
3. Add Liquid: Pour in the vegetable or chicken broth. Bring the mixture to a gentle boil, then reduce the heat to a simmer. Let it simmer for about 15-20 minutes, or until the broccoli is tender.
4. Blend the Mixture: Use an immersion blender or transfer the

mixture to a stand blender to puree until smooth.

5. Incorporate Dairy: Once the soup is smooth, return it to the pot if necessary. Pour in the whole milk or heavy cream, stirring to combine.

6. Add Gouda Cheese: Gradually add the shredded Gouda cheese to the soup, stirring until fully melted and incorporated.

7. Season and Serve: Taste the soup and season with salt and pepper as needed.

Achieving a Unique Flavor Profile

The incorporation of smoky Gouda cheese in this variation creates a flavor profile that's both distinct and delicious. Here's why Gouda is a perfect match for your broccoli soup:

Smokiness: Gouda cheese often has a mild smokiness that adds depth to the soup without overwhelming the other flavors.

Creamy Melting: Gouda has excellent melting qualities, ensuring that it blends seamlessly into the creamy soup base.

Complexity: The combination of Gouda's rich taste with the earthiness of broccoli results in a well-balanced and multidimensional dish.

Pairing with Bread or Crackers

To enhance your smoky Gouda and broccoli soup experience, consider pairing it with the following bread or cracker options:

Crusty Baguette: A classic choice, a slice of crusty baguette pairs beautifully with the creamy and smoky flavors of the soup.

Multigrain Bread: opt for multigrain or whole wheat bread for added texture and nutty undertones that complement the Gouda cheese.

Herb Crackers: A selection of herb-infused crackers can provide a delightful contrast in flavor and texture to the soup.

Cheese Straws: Elevate your pairing game with homemade or store-bought cheese straws, which mirror the cheese's essence.

By incorporating smoky Gouda into your broccoli cheddar soup, you're crafting a variation that's both sophisticated and comforting. The fusion of smokiness and creaminess results in a harmonious balance that's sure to satisfy your cravings for a unique and delectable culinary experience.

Chapter 11: Broccoli Cheddar Soup with Quinoa and Spinach

Adding Protein with Quinoa

Elevate your broccoli cheddar soup by incorporating quinoa, a protein-packed grain that adds both texture and nutritional value to the dish. This variation transforms the classic soup into a hearty and wholesome meal that's as filling as it is delicious.

Ingredients:

- 2 tablespoons olive oil
- 1 medium onion, diced
- 2 cloves garlic, minced
- 4 cups broccoli florets
- 3 cups vegetable or chicken broth
- 1 cup cooked quinoa
- 2 cups whole milk or heavy cream
- 1 ½ cups shredded sharp cheddar cheese
- Salt and pepper to taste

Instructions:

1. Sauté the Aromatics: Heat the olive oil in a large soup pot over medium heat. Add the diced onion and sauté until translucent, about 3-4 minutes. Stir in the minced garlic and sauté for an additional 1-2 minutes until fragrant.
2. Cook the Broccoli: Add the broccoli florets to the pot and sauté with the aromatics for about 5 minutes, allowing the flavors to meld.
3. Add Liquid: Pour in the vegetable or chicken broth. Bring the mixture to a gentle boil, then reduce the heat to a simmer. Let it simmer for about 15-20 minutes, or until the broccoli is tender.

4. Blend the Mixture: Use an immersion blender or transfer the mixture to a stand blender to puree until smooth.

5. Incorporate Quinoa: Stir in the cooked quinoa, adding a protein-rich element that enhances the soup's nutritional value and adds a delightful chewy texture.

6. Incorporate Dairy: Once the soup is smooth, return it to the pot if necessary. Pour in the whole milk or heavy cream, stirring to combine.

7. Add Cheese: Gradually add the shredded cheddar cheese to the soup, stirring until fully melted and incorporated.

8. Season and Serve: Taste the soup and season with salt and pepper as needed. Keep in mind that the cheese adds saltiness, so adjust accordingly.

Nutrient Boost from Spinach

Incorporating nutrient-rich spinach into your quinoa-infused broccoli cheddar soup adds a vibrant pop of color and a plethora of health benefits:

Iron and Vitamins: Spinach is an excellent source of iron, along with vitamins A and C, which contribute to overall well-being.

Vibrant Color: The bright green hue of spinach creates an appealing contrast in the soup, making it visually enticing.

Leafy Texture: The delicate leafy texture of spinach adds another layer of interest to the soup's overall mouthfeel.

Wholesome and Filling Soup Variation

By introducing quinoa and spinach, you're crafting a variation of broccoli cheddar soup that's both filling and nutritious:

Satiety Factor: The combination of quinoa's protein content and the fibrous goodness of broccoli and spinach makes this soup a satisfying and substantial meal.

Balanced Meal: With protein, vegetables, and grains all in one bowl, this soup provides a well-rounded combination of nutrients.

Texture Play: The tender broccoli, chewy quinoa, and leafy spinach create an engaging interplay of textures that keeps every spoonful interesting.

By incorporating quinoa and spinach into your broccoli cheddar soup, you're creating a variation that embraces wholesome ingredients while delivering a hearty and satisfying culinary experience.

Chapter 12: Italian-Inspired Broccoli and Parmesan Soup

Infusing Italian Flavors

Transport your taste buds to Italy with a Mediterranean-inspired twist on broccoli cheddar soup. This variation brings the rich and vibrant flavors of Italian cuisine to your bowl, creating a comforting and aromatic soup that's a delightful departure from the ordinary.

Ingredients:

- 2 tablespoons olive oil
- 1 medium onion, diced
- 2 cloves garlic, minced
- 4 cups broccoli florets
- 3 cups vegetable or chicken broth
- 1 cup whole milk or heavy cream
- 1 ½ cups grated Parmesan cheese
- 1 teaspoon dried basil
- 1 teaspoon dried oregano
- Salt and pepper to taste

Instructions:

1. Sauté the Aromatics: In a large soup pot, heat the olive oil over medium heat. Add the diced onion and sauté until translucent, about 3-4 minutes. Stir in the minced garlic and sauté for an additional 1-2 minutes until fragrant.
2. Cook the Broccoli: Add the broccoli florets to the pot and sauté with the aromatics for about 5 minutes, allowing the flavors to meld.
3. Add Liquid: Pour in the vegetable or chicken broth. Bring the mixture to a gentle boil, then reduce the heat to a simmer. Let it

simmer for about 15-20 minutes, or until the broccoli is tender.

4. Blend the Mixture: Use an immersion blender or transfer the mixture to a stand blender to puree until smooth.

5. Incorporate Dairy: Once the soup is smooth, return it to the pot if necessary. Pour in the whole milk or heavy cream, stirring to combine.

6. Add Parmesan Cheese: Gradually add the grated Parmesan cheese to the soup, stirring until fully melted and incorporated.

7. Infuse Italian Flavors: Stir in the dried basil and dried oregano, infusing the soup with the aromatic essence of Italian herbs.

8. Season and Serve: Taste the soup and season with salt and pepper as needed. Keep in mind that the Parmesan cheese adds saltiness, so adjust accordingly.

The Role of Parmesan Cheese

Parmesan cheese plays a starring role in this Italian-inspired variation, contributing to the distinct flavor profile of the soup:

Umami Depth: The savory notes of Parmesan cheese add a layer of umami that enhances the overall richness of the soup.

Saltiness and Creaminess: The cheese brings both saltiness and creaminess, creating a harmonious balance of flavors and textures.

Signature Flavor: Parmesan's nutty and slightly tangy taste is a hallmark of Italian cuisine and contributes to the authenticity of the dish.

Garnishing with Fresh Herbs

Elevate your Italian-inspired broccoli and Parmesan soup with the addition of fresh herbs as a garnish:

Fresh Basil: Tear or chop fresh basil leaves and sprinkle them on top of each bowl for a burst of vibrant flavor.

Chopped Parsley: Finely chop parsley and scatter it over the soup to add a fresh and herbaceous note.

Chives: Snip chives into small pieces and use them as a delicate garnish that enhances the visual appeal.

Herb-Infused Olive Oil: Drizzle a swirl of herb-infused olive oil over the soup just before serving for an extra layer of aromatic indulgence.

By infusing Italian flavors into your broccoli cheddar soup, you're creating a variation that transports you to the sun-drenched landscapes of Italy. The combination of Parmesan cheese and Mediterranean herbs results in a culinary masterpiece that's both comforting and captivating.

Chapter 13: Thai Coconut Broccoli Cheddar Soup

A Fusion of Flavors: Thai and Comfort

Embark on a culinary adventure with a fusion of Thai and comfort cuisine in this Thai Coconut Broccoli Cheddar Soup. This variation marries the rich and creamy essence of cheddar with the vibrant and aromatic flavors of Thai ingredients, resulting in a truly unforgettable bowl of soup.

Ingredients:

- 2 tablespoons vegetable oil
- 1 medium onion, diced
- 2 cloves garlic, minced
- 4 cups broccoli florets
- 3 cups vegetable or chicken broth
- 1 can (13.5 oz) coconut milk
- 1 ½ cups shredded sharp cheddar cheese
- 2 tablespoons Thai red curry paste
- 1 tablespoon brown sugar
- 2 tablespoons fish sauce (or soy sauce for a vegetarian version)
- Juice of 1 lime
- Salt and pepper to taste
- Fresh cilantro leaves for garnish
- Sliced red chili peppers for garnish

Instructions:

1. Sauté the Aromatics: Heat the vegetable oil in a large soup pot over medium heat. Add the diced onion and sauté until translucent, about 3-4 minutes. Stir in the minced garlic and

sauté for an additional 1-2 minutes until fragrant.

2. Cook the Broccoli: Add the broccoli florets to the pot and sauté with the aromatics for about 5 minutes, allowing the flavors to meld.

3. Add Liquid: Pour in the vegetable or chicken broth. Bring the mixture to a gentle boil, then reduce the heat to a simmer. Let it simmer for about 15-20 minutes, or until the broccoli is tender.

4. Blend the Mixture: Use an immersion blender or transfer the mixture to a stand blender to puree until smooth.

5. Incorporate Coconut Milk: Pour in the coconut milk, stirring to combine. The coconut milk adds a luscious creaminess and a hint of tropical flavor.

6. Add Cheddar Cheese: Gradually add the shredded cheddar cheese to the soup, stirring until fully melted and incorporated.

7. Introduce Thai Flavors: Stir in the Thai red curry paste, brown sugar, fish sauce (or soy sauce), and lime juice. These ingredients create a harmonious balance of sweet, sour, salty, and spicy flavors.

8. Balancing Flavors: Taste the soup and adjust the seasoning with salt and pepper if needed. Keep in mind that the fish sauce (or soy sauce) contributes saltiness to the dish.

Balancing Sweet, Sour, Salty, and Spicy

Incorporating Thai flavors into your broccoli cheddar soup involves achieving a delicate balance of the four key tastes that define Thai cuisine:

Sweetness: The brown sugar contributes a touch of sweetness that counterbalances the heat and enhances the overall flavor complexity.

Sourness: The lime juice adds a zesty and tangy note that brightens the flavors and provides a refreshing contrast.

Saltiness: The fish sauce (or soy sauce) brings a savory depth that complements the creamy base and adds depth to the soup.

Spiciness: The Thai red curry paste introduces a gentle spiciness that builds layers of complexity and warms the palate.

Garnishing with Fresh Herbs and Chilies

Elevate your Thai Coconut Broccoli Cheddar Soup by garnishing it with these vibrant and aromatic toppings:

Fresh Cilantro: Tear or chop fresh cilantro leaves and sprinkle them over the soup for a burst of herbal fragrance.

Sliced Red Chili Peppers: For an extra kick of heat and visual appeal, add thinly sliced red chili peppers on top.

By combining the comfort of cheddar cheese with the exotic allure of Thai flavors, you're crafting a soup that tantalizes the taste buds and transports you to the vibrant streets of Thailand. This fusion of cuisines offers a culinary experience that's both comforting and adventurous.

Chapter 14: Broccoli Cheddar Soup with Herbed Croutons

Homemade Herbed Croutons

Take your broccoli cheddar soup to the next level by pairing it with homemade herbed croutons. These golden nuggets of flavor and crunch add a delightful dimension to the soup, elevating both taste and texture.

Ingredients for Herbed Croutons:

- 4 cups day-old bread cubes (baguette, ciabatta, or sourdough)
- 2 tablespoons olive oil
- 1 teaspoon dried thyme
- 1 teaspoon dried rosemary
- 1 teaspoon dried oregano
- Salt and pepper to taste

Instructions for Herbed Croutons:

1. Preheat the Oven: Preheat your oven to 375°F (190°C).
2. Prepare the Bread Cubes: Cut the day-old bread into bite-sized cubes. Ensure they are relatively uniform in size for even toasting.
3. Season the Croutons: In a mixing bowl, combine the olive oil, dried thyme, dried rosemary, dried oregano, salt, and pepper. Toss the bread cubes in this mixture, ensuring they are well coated.
4. Toast the Croutons: Spread the seasoned bread cubes on a baking sheet in a single layer. Toast them in the preheated oven for about 10-15 minutes or until they turn golden brown and crispy. Be sure to toss them around halfway through for even toasting.
5. Cool and Store: Allow the croutons to cool completely before

using them as a garnish for your soup. You can store any extra croutons in an airtight container for future use.

Crunch and Flavor Contrast

The addition of herbed croutons brings an exciting contrast to your broccoli cheddar soup:

Texture Play: The crispiness of the croutons creates an engaging textural contrast against the creamy soup base.

Herbaceous Ness: The blend of dried thyme, rosemary, and oregano infuses the croutons with a fragrant herbaceous flavor that complements the soup's richness.

Enhanced Flavor: The herbed croutons add an extra layer of taste to each spoonful, enhancing the overall flavor experience.

Elevating Presentation

Incorporating herbed croutons not only enhances the taste of your broccoli cheddar soup but also elevates its visual appeal:

Artful Arrangement: Sprinkle a handful of herbed croutons on top of each bowl of soup in an artful arrangement. This not only adds visual interest but also showcases the attention to detail.

Croutons on the Side: Alternatively, serve the herbed croutons in a separate bowl alongside the soup, allowing diners to customize their own portions.

Crouton Variety: Experiment with different types of bread for your croutons, such as whole grain, sourdough, or rye, to introduce diverse flavors and textures.

By adding homemade herbed croutons to your broccoli cheddar soup, you're creating a culinary experience that engages all the senses. The interplay of creaminess and crunch, along with the aromatic herbs, adds depth to your soup and elevates its presentation to a gourmet level.

Chapter 15: Kid-Friendly Cheesy Broccoli Soup Bites

Mini Versions for Kids

Introduce a playful twist to your broccoli cheddar soup by creating adorable and delicious kid-friendly cheesy broccoli soup bites. These bite-sized treats are designed to capture the hearts of little ones while ensuring they enjoy a nutritious meal.

Ingredients for Cheesy Broccoli Soup Bites:

- 2 cups broccoli florets, finely chopped
- 1 cup cooked and mashed potatoes
- 1 cup shredded cheddar cheese
- ¼ cup whole milk or vegetable broth (as needed for consistency)
- Salt and pepper to taste
- Cooking spray or olive oil

Instructions for Cheesy Broccoli Soup Bites:

1. Prepare the Broccoli: Steam or blanch the broccoli florets until tender. Finely chop them into small pieces.
2. Mash the Potatoes: Cook and mash the potatoes until they are smooth and free of lumps.
3. Combine Ingredients: In a mixing bowl, combine the chopped broccoli, mashed potatoes, shredded cheddar cheese, and a small amount of milk or vegetable broth. Mix until you achieve a thick yet manageable consistency. Season with salt and pepper.
4. Shape the Bites: Using your hands or a spoon, shape the mixture into bite-sized portions. You can create fun shapes like small balls, mini patties, or even use cookie cutters for playful designs.
5. Cook the Bites: Preheat a non-stick skillet over medium heat

and lightly coat it with cooking spray or a drizzle of olive oil. Place the shaped bites on the skillet and cook for 2-3 minutes on each side, or until they turn golden brown and crispy.

6. Serve and Enjoy: Allow the cheesy broccoli soup bites to cool slightly before serving them to your little ones. These bites are perfect for dipping into the full-sized broccoli cheddar soup for a fun and flavorful experience.

Creative Shapes and Fun Presentation

The key to enticing kids is presenting food in creative and visually appealing ways:

Shape Variety: Experiment with different shapes, sizes, and designs for the soup bites. Use cookie cutters to create stars, hearts, animals, or any other shapes that spark their imagination.

Colorful Presentation: Serve the cheesy broccoli soup bites on colorful plates or with dipping sauces to enhance the overall presentation.

Dipping Sauces: Offer small bowls of mild dipping sauces, such as ranch dressing or yogurt-based dips, to make the experience even more enjoyable for kids.

Getting Kids to Enjoy Veggies

By transforming broccoli cheddar soup into fun and bite-sized portions, you're making it easier for kids to embrace vegetables:

Texture Appeal: The crispy exterior and tender interior of the bites provide a pleasant textural contrast that's likely to win over young palates.

Interactive Eating: Kids love interactive eating experiences. Encourage them to dip the bites into their soup for a playful and engaging meal.

Hidden Nutrition: Sneaking mashed potatoes and chopped broccoli into the bites adds an extra dose of nutrients, making the dish even more wholesome.

By creating kid-friendly cheesy broccoli soup bites, you're fostering a positive relationship between children and vegetables while making mealtime a joyful and delightful affair.

Chapter 16: Rustic Broccoli Cheddar Soup with Country Bread

Serving Inside Bread Bowls

Elevate your broccoli cheddar soup experience by serving it within hearty and edible bread bowls. This rustic presentation not only adds a touch of charm but also transforms your soup into a complete and satisfying meal.

Ingredients for Bread Bowls:

- 4 round country bread loaves (sourdough, rustic, or whole grain)
- Butter for brushing (optional)

Instructions for Bread Bowls:

1. Prepare the Bread Loaves: Using a serrated knife, carefully cut the tops off the bread loaves. Hollow out the centers, leaving about a 1-inch thick border to form bowls. Reserve the removed bread for making croutons or breadcrumbs.
2. Brush with Butter (Optional): If desired, brush the inside of the bread bowls with melted butter. This step adds flavor and helps create a barrier to prevent the soup from making the bread too soggy.
3. Toast the Bread Bowls: Preheat your oven to 350°F (175°C). Place the bread bowls, including the tops, on a baking sheet and toast them in the oven for about 5-7 minutes, or until they turn slightly golden and crisp. Keep an eye on them to avoid over-browning.
4. Fill with Soup: Ladle the prepared rustic broccoli cheddar soup into the bread bowls, filling them generously.
5. Serve and Enjoy: Replace the tops of the bread bowls and serve

immediately. Encourage diners to dip pieces of the bread bowl into the soup as they enjoy this comforting and satisfying meal.

Complementing with Rustic Bread

Pairing your broccoli cheddar soup with rustic bread bowls creates a harmonious culinary experience:

Flavorful Union: The earthy and hearty flavors of rustic bread complement the rich and creamy profile of the soup.

Textural Balance: The crusty exterior of the bread contrasts beautifully with the smoothness of the soup, adding an enjoyable textural interplay.

Serving Convenience: The bread bowl serves as both a vessel for the soup and a convenient way to enjoy every last drop.

Cozy and Satisfying Meal

Serving your broccoli cheddar soup in rustic bread bowls adds an element of comfort and satisfaction:

Enhanced Presentation: The sight of soup-filled bread bowls exudes warmth and rustic charm, making the dining experience feel cozy and inviting.

One-Pot Meal: The combination of soup and bread in a single bowl creates a self-contained meal that's perfect for enjoying on chilly days or when seeking comfort.

Nostalgic Appeal: Bread bowls evoke memories of comforting meals enjoyed at home or in cozy eateries, making the experience even more enjoyable.

By serving your rustic broccoli cheddar soup inside country bread bowls, you're offering a unique and hearty dining experience that's as delightful as it is delicious.

Chapter 17: Mediterranean Feta and Broccoli Soup

Incorporating Mediterranean Ingredients

Transport your taste buds to the shores of the Mediterranean with a tantalizing fusion of flavors in this Mediterranean Feta and Broccoli Soup. By infusing the soup with ingredients reminiscent of the Mediterranean cuisine, you're creating a dish that's both exotic and comforting.

Ingredients:

- 2 tablespoons olive oil
- 1 medium onion, diced
- 2 cloves garlic, minced
- 4 cups broccoli florets
- 3 cups vegetable or chicken broth
- 1 cup whole milk or heavy cream
- 1 cup crumbled feta cheese
- ½ cup sliced Kalamata olives
- 2 tablespoons chopped fresh basil
- 1 tablespoon chopped fresh oregano
- Salt and pepper to taste

Instructions:

1. Sauté the Aromatics: In a large soup pot, heat the olive oil over medium heat. Add the diced onion and sauté until translucent, about 3-4 minutes. Stir in the minced garlic and sauté for an additional 1-2 minutes until fragrant.
2. Cook the Broccoli: Add the broccoli florets to the pot and sauté with the aromatics for about 5 minutes, allowing the flavors to meld.

3. Add Liquid: Pour in the vegetable or chicken broth. Bring the mixture to a gentle boil, then reduce the heat to a simmer. Let it simmer for about 15-20 minutes, or until the broccoli is tender.

4. Blend the Mixture: Use an immersion blender or transfer the mixture to a stand blender to puree until smooth.

5. Incorporate Dairy: Once the soup is smooth, return it to the pot if necessary. Pour in the whole milk or heavy cream, stirring to combine.

6. Add Feta Cheese: Gradually add the crumbled feta cheese to the soup, stirring until fully melted and incorporated.

7. Introduce Mediterranean Flavors: Stir in the sliced Kalamata olives, chopped fresh basil, and chopped fresh oregano. These ingredients infuse the soup with the vibrant and aromatic essence of the Mediterranean.

8. Season and Serve: Taste the soup and season with salt and pepper as needed. Keep in mind that the feta cheese and olives contribute saltiness to the dish.

Creaminess from Feta Cheese

The crumbled feta cheese not only adds creaminess but also contributes to the Mediterranean flavor profile:

Tangy Creaminess: Feta's tangy and slightly salty profile enhances the overall richness of the soup while adding a Mediterranean twist.

Texture Variation: The crumbled feta cheese introduces delightful pockets of creamy texture and bursts of flavor to each spoonful.

Olives, Herbs, and Mediterranean Touches

By incorporating olives, fresh herbs, and other Mediterranean elements, you're crafting a soup that's a feast for both the palate and the senses:

Kalamata Olives: The briny and fruity notes of Kalamata olives bring a unique depth to the soup, echoing the flavors of Mediterranean cuisine.

Fresh Basil and Oregano: The fragrant aroma and earthy taste of fresh basil and oregano contribute a vibrant and herbaceous layer to the dish.

Mediterranean Vibes: The combination of olives, herbs, and feta cheese captures the essence of the Mediterranean, offering a taste of sunny coastal regions.

By infusing your broccoli cheddar soup with Mediterranean flavors, you're creating a variation that celebrates the richness of cultural culinary influences. The fusion of feta, olives, and herbs results in a soup that's both comforting and transportive, evoking the spirit of the Mediterranean with every spoonful.

Chapter 18: Creamy Broccoli Cheddar Soup with Turmeric

Health Benefits of Turmeric

Elevate your broccoli cheddar soup's nutritional profile by infusing it with the golden goodness of turmeric. This vibrant spice boasts numerous health benefits, making your soup not only delicious but also a nourishing treat for the body.

Ingredients:

- 2 tablespoons butter
- 1 medium onion, diced
- 2 cloves garlic, minced
- 4 cups broccoli florets
- 3 cups vegetable or chicken broth
- 2 cups whole milk or heavy cream
- 1 ½ cups shredded sharp cheddar cheese
- 1 teaspoon ground turmeric
- ½ teaspoon ground cumin
- ¼ teaspoon ground coriander
- Salt and pepper to taste

Instructions:

1. Sauté the Aromatics: In a large soup pot, melt the butter over medium heat. Add the diced onion and sauté until translucent, about 3-4 minutes. Stir in the minced garlic and sauté for an additional 1-2 minutes until fragrant.
2. Cook the Broccoli: Add the broccoli florets to the pot and sauté with the aromatics for about 5 minutes, allowing the flavors to meld.
3. Add Liquid: Pour in the vegetable or chicken broth. Bring the

mixture to a gentle boil, then reduce the heat to a simmer. Let it simmer for about 15-20 minutes, or until the broccoli is tender.

4. Blend the Mixture: Use an immersion blender or transfer the mixture to a stand blender to puree until smooth.

5. Incorporate Dairy: Once the soup is smooth, return it to the pot if necessary. Pour in the whole milk or heavy cream, stirring to combine.

6. Add Cheddar Cheese: Gradually add the shredded cheddar cheese to the soup, stirring until fully melted and incorporated.

7. Introduce Turmeric and Spices: Stir in the ground turmeric, ground cumin, and ground coriander. These spices add a vibrant color and earthy depth to the soup.

8. Season and Serve: Taste the soup and season with salt and pepper as needed. The turmeric, along with the cheese and spices, adds a unique flavor profile.

Adding Color and Earthy Flavor

The addition of turmeric not only enhances the health benefits but also imparts a rich color and depth of flavor to your broccoli cheddar soup:

Golden Hue: Turmeric's distinct yellow color gives the soup a beautiful and inviting appearance.

Earthy Notes: The combination of ground cumin and coriander alongside the turmeric adds a warm and earthy undertone that complements the creaminess of the soup.

Immune-Boosting Twist

Turmeric is known for its immune-boosting and anti-inflammatory properties:

Curcumin Power: The active compound in turmeric, curcumin, is believed to have potent antioxidant and anti-inflammatory effects that support overall health.

Wellness Booster: By incorporating turmeric into your soup, you're adding an extra layer of wellness to your meal.

By infusing your broccoli cheddar soup with the goodness of turmeric, you're creating a variation that not only delights your taste buds but also supports your well-being. The vibrant color, earthy flavors, and immune-boosting properties of turmeric turn your soup into a comforting and nourishing experience.

Chapter 19: Broccoli Cheddar Soup for the Instant Pot

Utilizing the Instant Pot's Convenience

Harness the power of the Instant Pot to whip up a delectable broccoli cheddar soup in no time. The Instant Pot's convenience and efficiency make this variation a perfect choice for busy days when you're craving a comforting and satisfying meal.

Ingredients:

- 2 tablespoons butter
- 1 medium onion, diced
- 2 cloves garlic, minced
- 4 cups broccoli florets
- 3 cups vegetable or chicken broth
- 1 cup whole milk or heavy cream
- 1 ½ cups shredded sharp cheddar cheese
- Salt and pepper to taste

Instructions:

1. Sauté in Instant Pot: Set your Instant Pot to the "Sauté" mode. Melt the butter and add the diced onion. Sauté until translucent, about 3-4 minutes. Stir in the minced garlic and sauté for an additional 1-2 minutes until fragrant.
2. Cook the Broccoli: Add the broccoli florets to the Instant Pot and sauté briefly with the aromatics.
3. Add Liquid: Pour in the vegetable or chicken broth. Cancel the "Sauté" mode. Close the Instant Pot lid and ensure the vent is set to "Sealing."
4. Pressure Cook: Select the "Pressure Cook" or "Manual" mode and set the timer for 5 minutes on high pressure.

5. Quick Release and Blend: Once the cooking time is complete, carefully perform a quick release of pressure. Use an immersion blender directly in the Instant Pot to puree the mixture until smooth.

6. Incorporate Dairy: Set the Instant Pot to the "Sauté" mode again. Pour in the whole milk or heavy cream, stirring to combine.

7. Add Cheddar Cheese: Gradually add the shredded cheddar cheese to the soup, stirring until fully melted and incorporated.

8. Season and Serve: Taste the soup and season with salt and pepper as needed. The cheese adds saltiness, so adjust accordingly.

Adjusting Cooking Times and Methods

When adapting recipes for the Instant Pot, it's essential to make adjustments to cooking times and methods:

Sauté Mode: The Instant Pot's "Sauté" mode is ideal for sautéing aromatics before pressure cooking, adding depth of flavor to your soup.

Pressure Cook Time: Broccoli cooks quickly under pressure. A short pressure cook time of 5 minutes ensures tender broccoli without overcooking it.

Quick Release: Using the quick release method allows you to halt cooking immediately, preventing overcooking and preserving the vibrant color of the broccoli.

Quick and Flavorful Results

The Instant Pot's efficiency delivers exceptional results while saving you time:

Time-Saving: The Instant Pot's pressure cooking feature accelerates the cooking process, making this variation perfect for quick weeknight meals.

Flavorful Fusion: Despite the shortened cooking time, the melding of flavors is no compromise. The cheese, aromatics, and broccoli still infuse the soup with exceptional taste.

Consistent Creaminess: The Instant Pot's precise pressure cooking ensures that the soup achieves the desired creamy consistency.

By utilizing the Instant Pot's convenience, you're making cooking simpler and more efficient while still enjoying the rich and comforting flavors of broccoli cheddar soup. This variation caters to busy lifestyles without compromising on taste and quality.

Chapter 20: Gluten-Free Broccoli Cheddar Soup with Almond Flour Roux

Roux Alternatives for Gluten-Free Diets

For those following a gluten-free diet, making a roux—the traditional thickening agent—can be a challenge. Fear not! With the use of almond flour, you can achieve the same luxurious thickness and indulgence in your broccoli cheddar soup while keeping it completely gluten-free.

Ingredients:

- 2 tablespoons butter
- 1 medium onion, diced
- 2 cloves garlic, minced
- 4 cups broccoli florets
- 3 cups vegetable or chicken broth
- 1 cup whole milk or heavy cream
- 1 ½ cups shredded sharp cheddar cheese
- ¼ cup almond flour
- Salt and pepper to taste

Instructions:

1. Sauté the Aromatics: In a large soup pot, melt the butter over medium heat. Add the diced onion and sauté until translucent, about 3-4 minutes. Stir in the minced garlic and sauté for an additional 1-2 minutes until fragrant.
2. Cook the Broccoli: Add the broccoli florets to the pot and sauté with the aromatics for about 5 minutes, allowing the flavors to meld.
3. Add Liquid: Pour in the vegetable or chicken broth. Bring the mixture to a gentle boil, then reduce the heat to a simmer. Let it

simmer for about 15-20 minutes, or until the broccoli is tender.

4. Blend the Mixture: Use an immersion blender or transfer the mixture to a stand blender to puree until smooth.

5. Incorporate Dairy: Once the soup is smooth, return it to the pot if necessary. Pour in the whole milk or heavy cream, stirring to combine.

6. Add Cheddar Cheese: Gradually add the shredded cheddar cheese to the soup, stirring until fully melted and incorporated.

7. Thicken with Almond Flour Roux: In a separate small skillet, toast the almond flour over medium heat for a couple of minutes until it turns slightly golden and fragrant. Add the toasted almond flour to the soup, stirring constantly to create a roux-like thickening effect. Continue to cook for a few minutes until the soup reaches your desired thickness.

8. Season and Serve: Taste the soup and season with salt and pepper as needed. The cheese adds saltiness, so adjust accordingly.

Achieving Thickness with Almond Flour

Almond flour is an excellent gluten-free alternative to traditional roux. It provides a creamy consistency and nutty flavor that complements the soup:

Roux Replacement: Almond flour acts as a roux, thickening the soup to a velvety consistency without the need for wheat-based flour.

Nutty Accent: The almond flour brings a subtle nutty flavor that pairs harmoniously with the broccoli and cheddar.

Catering to Dietary Needs without Compromising Flavor

Gluten-free eating can be both delicious and satisfying:

Gluten-Free Indulgence: This variation ensures that those with gluten sensitivities can enjoy the same rich and creamy experience.

Flavor Uncompromised: The almond flour roux not only thickens but also imparts a pleasing texture and enhances the overall flavor profile.

Inclusive Dining: Whether you follow a gluten-free diet or not, this version appeals to all palates.

By using almond flour to thicken your broccoli cheddar soup, you're creating a variation that's both gluten-free and scrumptiously indulgent. This ensures that everyone can savor the comfort of this classic soup without any dietary limitations getting in the way.

In this culinary journey through "Broccoli Cheddar Soup Recipes," we've explored a diverse range of variations that cater to different tastes, preferences, and dietary needs. From classic creamy soups to innovative twists, each chapter has been a celebration of creativity and comfort.

Whether you're a fan of traditional flavors or eager to experiment with new ingredients, this cookbook has provided you with a comprehensive guide to crafting delicious broccoli cheddar soups that delight the senses. Each recipe has been thoughtfully crafted to ensure a balance of taste, texture, and visual appeal.

As you embark on your soup-making adventures, remember that cooking is a creative process, and these recipes serve as a foundation for your culinary exploration. Feel free to personalize and adapt the recipes to your liking, experiment with different combinations, and add your unique touch to each dish.

May your kitchen be filled with the enticing aroma of simmering soups, and may each spoonful bring warmth and joy to your taste buds. Whether you're preparing a cozy family dinner or impressing guests with your culinary prowess, these broccoli cheddar soup recipes are your gateway to a world of comfort and flavor.

Happy cooking, and bon appétit!

www.ingramcontent.com/pod-product-compliance
Lightning Source LLC
Chambersburg PA
CBHW031424160726

47993CB00003B/1380